PAINTING OF THE WESTERN WORLD

THE ITALIAN RENAISSANCE

PAINTING OF THE WESTERN WORLD

THE ITALIAN RENAISSANCE

by Ian Barras Hill

Galley Press

Library of Congress Catalog Card No.
79-5367
ISBN 0-8317 4495 2
Manufactured in the Netherlands

Contents

Color illustrations

CHAPTER I

The rebirth of passion

The Renaissance - Seminal time for painting - Rejection of medievalism - Awakening of imagination - Inspiration of Classical times - Limitation of religious subject matter - Audacity of Renaissance painters - Renaissance painting as an illustration of the age - Roots of the Renaissance - Cimabue and Giotto - Stagnation after Giotto - Brunelleschi and Donatello meet Masaccio.

David, 1440-42
bronze by Donatello
Florence, Museo Nazionale

If we look back through the history of Western art for the one decisive movement which precipitated all the familiar paintings displayed in Western galleries, we look back to the Renaissance. The Italian Renaissance – once a narrow term referring to the revival of Latin literature and of a classical style in the arts – has come to mean an explosive period in European history that began in Italy in the 15th century as a reaction to medieval values and spread over the Alps to Northern Europe, although there is evidence of a similar spontaneous rejection of medievalism elsewhere, especially in Flanders. The movement came as a quickening of the imagination, a new and daring respect for human personality; a springtime of awakening passion after a winter of dormant feeling through the dark years of medieval Christian belief.

In order to justify abandoning religious authority in favour of human values, the artists and intellectuals of the Renaissance looked back over a thousand years of barren medievalism to the classical times of ancient Greece and Rome, when poetry and sculpture expressed individual human feeling. With this inspiration, and within a century, Italian painting moved away from stylized and decorative portraits of the Madonna and saints in Byzantine colours to the paintings of delicate ambiguity by Leonardo da Vinci, such as the portraits of Ginevra de Benci or of the Mona Lisa – portraits which depict confident personalities who seem to hint to us some potent sexual knowledge with their knowing, almost insolent, smiles. And within decades the movement led to the final flourish of the Renaissance, to a style called Mannerism where the paintings of fleshy and intense realism by Michelangelo and Parmigianino became so sensuous and disturbing in their depiction of facial expression, muscled torsoes and active limbs that they remain, for many, exaggerated, operatic and even sinister.

Although we are concerned with the Renaissance as a movement in painting which spanned two centuries, from 1400-1600, it was, more significantly, a far-reaching cultural evolution in which the developments in painting had only a limited impact on the cultures of other continents. Far more important was the parallel development in self-awareness called Humanism, which brought a new respect for man, with his passions and his intellect, and saw him as something far more than a mechanical puppet of a hidden God. Humanism was developed by a new breed of intellectuals and artists who flourished outside of religious institutions. They did not regard human personality as something to be tamed and suppressed. They delighted in man as a being of emotion and reason. The paintings and frescoes by Masaccio brought a new sense of man, anatomically convincing, emotionally disturbing – portraits of flesh and feeling that induced sympathy in the minds of those who saw them.

A new interest in intelligent, literate, articulate man hastened the development and spread of painting and of literacy as a secular activity, where previously it had been a monopoly of the church. The growth of cities brought about the complex structures of law

Dome of the S. Maria del Fiore
in Florence, 1420-36
by Filippo Brunelleschi

8

and government, often borrowing from Roman models, and this triggered public debates on politics and public morality. With growing confidence the countries now affected by a new curiosity financed explorations around Africa, and the voyages which led to the discovery of the Americas. Freedom from the dogma of religious authority brought about an analytical, enquiring approach to the way society works, to astronomy, to the physical world, to clouds and the weather, to mechanical things, to plants and animals and to the way the human body works. The revelations of anatomical dissections, of the arrangements of feathers in the wings of a bird, of the way water flows or cloth falls into folds, all fed new confidence back to the painters of the human body. Once it began the Renaissance seemed self-generating. It fuelled itself in an unprecedented rush of progress in every area of human concern. Many intellectuals of the time became so enthused with the varieties of new knowledge that they indulged in many disciplines and became experts in a range of skills – commissioned to design a cathedral in one city, a military installation in another. Many Renaissance artists were versatile and had reputations in widely distinct disciplines. For his contributions to the arts and sciences, to aviation, mechanics, military engineering and to many lesser crafts Leonardo is the most renowned genius of his time, perhaps of all time. His few paintings, many unfinished, continue to claim as much attention as those of the far more prolific Michelangelo.

Most of the Renaissance paintings have been surpassed in aesthetic quality by later artists because the spirit of medievalism lingered, particularly in their choice of subject matter. There remains an excess of Madonnas and Saints, of Annunciations and "Agonies in the Garden". While it is illuminating to compare the treatment by different artists of the same theme, a modern view must necessarily be without the intense religious sympathies the painter brought to his subject matter. We no longer feel the same emotions about religious events; we no longer regard them as part of our personal history. Since the scientific theories of our evolution have taken hold, the stories of Adam and Eve or Noah have been reduced to less than potent myths.

Several of the Renaissance painters have never been equalled in the part they have played in the creative interpretation of sacred and secular events, or in the audacity of their conceptions. It must have required a rare confidence to paint in public the history of the world, the face of God, the bloody murder of the Saints or details of a mythological scene of carnal intimacy. The churches were left overflowing with nudity, which prompted later generations to paint clothes over some of the figures. For over a century the works of the Renaissance painters became a form of commentary, a revelation and finally an exaggeration of human feelings. They remain an illustration to the age: confident, intellectual and personal.

It is always misleading to imagine that a new movement of art came into being spontaneously, like an unexpected flowering of human genius in a wilderness of caution and sterility. Of course the

9

Self portrait, detail from the Gate
of Paradise, 1425-52
bronze by Lorenzo Ghiberti
Florence, Baptistry

roots of the Renaissance were quietly growing through the late Middle Ages. Long before the "official" date for the beginning of the Renaissance of about 1400, the foundations of a humanising art were being laid by Cimabue and Giotto.

Cimabue was the outstanding Florentine painter of the end of the 13th century. He tried by the use of imagination and a regard for reality to break with the stylized forms of Gothic art, and he made some small progress. Giotto was almost certainly his pupil and brought his own genius to the skills of drawing and the depiction of interesting character he had learned from Cimabue.

Giotto's particular skills consisted in bringing forward the neglected human personality in the figures of his religious frescoes. Details of clothes and locations are suborned to the more dramatic revelation of human personality through postures, glances and gestures. The figures come alive and tell a story. They have recognisable anatomies and are set in a simple kind of perspective. It must have seemed that Giotto had mastered painting, and indeed for eighty years after his death in 1337 the art of painting stagnated because his imitators drew upon his designs without caring much for his revolutionary principles. It was the influence of a sculptor and an architect which set the art of painting moving once more, and it was in Florence that the synthesis occurred.

Brunelleschi is best remembered as the architect of the Cathedral Dome in Florence, that most conspicuous landmark over the city. It is in fact two concrete domes, and the curious can crawl about in the medieval dust between the two.

It says something for the virtuosity of Renaissance man that he was an architect as an afterthought. He began his career as a goldsmith and sculptor, was a mechanic and inventor, made clocks, designed pumps, perused mathematics and most importantly he rediscovered the rules of scientific perspective which were known to the Greeks and Romans but lost again. This seminal discovery was a critical factor in the flowering of Renaissance painting.

Brunelleschi may well have moved to a career in architecture because in 1402 he lost a competition to make the bronze reliefs for the door of the Baptistery close to the Cathedral of Florence. The winner was Ghiberti whose bronze doors still delight the crowds these centuries later.

Within five years of this commission Ghiberti took on an apprentice in his workshop a young sculptor, Donatello, who had a deep passion for classical sculpture. As he mastered his art, Donatello was able to give a force and vitality to his sculpture and bronze reliefs which astonished the painters of the time. He modelled the first free-standing nude statue since antiquity, a bronze *David* which was later eclipsed by another David by Michelangelo. Renaissance painting may be said to have started by an association between Donatello, Brunelleschi and a young painter, moved up from the country, called Masaccio.

CHAPTER II

Founding fathers

Masaccio the fresco-painter – Castagno's "David" – Alberti's book on perspective and re-estimation of the artist – Transitional painters – Uccello and foreshortening – Veneziano and Venetian sense of colour – Fra Angelico – Benozzo Gozzoli – The celebrated Fra Filippo Lippi

Born in 1401 and living only to the age of 27, Masaccio the fresco painter blazed like a jewel, adorned his age and enlightened his contemporaries on new directions in painting style. He is the undisputed father of Renaissance painting, and all the Florentine masters of the Renaissance who came after him looked upon his wallpaintings as the definitive expression of Humanistic Man. He alone took the themes and fresco techniques of Giotto and breathed life into the figures, giving them not just animation and a human appearance, but also emotions! Massaccio's figures are actors caught in a moment of high drama. They are individuals; solid, beset with shadows and displayed in a scene of depth and perspective. His famous fresco of Adam and Eve expelled from Paradise portrays an emotionally distraught pair, ashamed of their nakedness and hurrying away from the wrath of God. Adam bows his head and covers his face in shame. Eve furrows her eyebrows and howls! Such passion unveiled in a holy event sent other artists to reinterpret Biblical scenes with equal vigour, and with appropriate melodrama.

The inspiration of investing the figures with emotions was taken up by the younger Andrea del Castagno (1421/3-57) whose portrait of the young David (1450) painted on the leather shape of a tournament shield, has the face of a man caught in the throes of emotional exhaustion, his hand raised to the skies in triumph, and the improbable head of Goliath between his feet. It is a brilliant creative interpretation of David, the man.

Masaccio was not only master of the one effect of emotionalism. He perused the causes of composition, realism and perspective. With an intuitive feel for perspective that recalls Donatello, Masaccio's frescoes of *The Tribute Money* (c. 1425) illustrates his ability to portray a group of figures with a new realism. The figures relate to one another, and argue among themselves. They are individuals and are moving among each other. The figures are larger than life and the painting is given depth by the trick of having figures approaching, or receding into the picture.

The Trinity, a fresco of about 1426-27 is the first recorded example of strict linear perspective used in fresco painting. The barrel vault of the hall recedes over the head of Christ as if the wall on which the fresco was painted had depth. The figures have real faces as if they were copied from people in the streets, and the

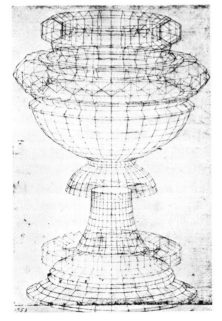

Perspective study of a chalice
drawing by Paolo Uccello
Florence, Galleria degli Uffizi

whole painting is lit in a natural way as if a painted sun were out of sight above the picture giving it a natural illumination. The presence of the arch in the painting indicates a desire to keep in touch with what was considered the classical model for humanist painting, Imperial Rome.

Overcoming the problem of perspective (understanding the rules by which objects recede into the picture to give it depth) was a considerable breakthrough for Renaissance painting with its representational quality, after the earlier Gothic painting which filled the canvas or board with fussy detail and unrealistic colours such as a gold sky. Sassetta (d. 1450), not a Florentine but from Siena, attempted to fuse the old Gothic style with the new Renaissance respect for character and perspective. His *St Francis Renounces his Earthly Father* of 1437-44 came at the peak of his career. It demonstrates a sophisticated colour sense and a bold disposition of his figures, but his attempt to indicate perspective with receding pillars confuses the eye so that indoors and out seem to interchange as we look at it, and we are troubled by the lack of shadow. Though he was influenced by the Florentine discoveries, he could not abandon his Gothic tradition.

About the time of Sassetta's *St Francis* a book by Leon Battista Alberti came into print whch clarified the problem. Called *Della Pittura* (On Painting), it was not just another book on how to mix paint, but a systematic approach to the problem of perspective, taken from Brunelleschi's researches. The book explained the astonishing truth that the observer's height and position when looking at a painting is controlled by the painter's use of perspective. It proposed that there is a set of rules that would allow a perspective to be built up in a painting which perfectly recreates the natural perspective we see in all three dimensional space. Flat paintings can simulate depth.

Apart from his mastery of perspective, the Renaissance genius Alberti – also poet, mapmaker and architect – expressed a growing respect for the painter, not just as a technician, but as a creator who had to choose, measure, arrange and harmonize the elements of his painting. He demonstrated painting to be an intellectual art by comparisons with the other liberal arts, and he spoke of art as a discipline that can be learned. All this contributed to the confidence of artists and their revaluation in society. The painter was becoming a hero; respected and trusted.

The Early Renaissance, 1420-1500, was characterized not by a unifying style, but by many personal styles as each artist struggled to break with the past and make use of the new techniques. Many artists tried the impossible; to reconcile the two. Uccello was trained in the workshop of Ghiberti, at the same time as Masaccio. His style was one of bright colours and the decorative arrangement of figures like toy soldiers on a board. He had an undeserved reputation for his handling of perspective but there's much of the old Gothic sense of tapestry, with the middle distance rearing up toward us as if the board of soldiers has been tilted forward. His three panels depicting the Battle of *San Romano* (c. 1456) now distributed among several galleries, were made to be decorative

Sir John Hawkwood, known as Giovanni Acuto, 1436
fresco by Paolo Uccello
Florence, S. Maria del Fiore

Facade of the S. Maria Novella
in Florence, completed in 1456
by Leone Battista Alberti

wall panels. He did not seem to aim for a naturalistic and random
distribution of people, horses, dogs or lances, but set them in
clusters and patterns in a state of Gothic formality.

The figures in Uccello's fresco *The Flood* (c. 1447) seem to be
influenced by Masaccio's famous figures.

Though Uccello's paintings are childlike and fussy they are
free from the emotionally-demanding style of his contemporaries
and have considerable charm in their distorted and almost comic
detail. He had a great influence on Florentine chestpainting, and
on Botticelli.

It was a Venetian, Domenico Veneziano, who arrived in Florence
and lightened the generally dark mood of painting. Under his
hand the colours softened to pale pinks and greens, and gave a
lighter complexion to painting. He took a new line on perspective,
bringing the horizon down so that we seem to view from the
height of a child, and the figures tower over us. *The Sacra
Conversazione* of the St Lucy altarpiece (1442-48) has a pleasing
array of figures in natural postures, though the stark face of
St John on the left takes us away from the delicate Madonna.
This panel has a harmony and balance, and is subtly illuminated
with a soft flow of sunshine above the Madonna's head which
fills the painting with light and shade. Veneziano passed on his
technique to his pupil Piero della Francesca.

Florence by the mid-15th century abounded with fresco and panel
painters. Each seemed a master in his art, only to be overtaken by
a pupil. Fra Angelico, a Dominican monk born in 1400, collabora-
ted with his pupil Gozzoli on many frescoes. By all accounts a
saintly man, he kept with the religious subjects but worked upon
the detail with a fine hand, and spread colour with great thought-
fulness to the accidents of light and shade in folds of cloth or
the contours of the face. In his fresco of *Pope Sixtus II giving the*

Warriors and horses, detail of the
Defeat of Chosroes, 1459
fresco by Piero della Francesca
Arezzo, S. Francesco

Church Treasure (1447-50) we can appreciate the tensions of the
scene and ignore the fact that the pursuing soldiers stand an
armslength from the Pope, and yet they do not see each other!
It might have been the flaw of most religious painting, that
villains were painted with greater realism, and tended to steal the
scene from the saints.

The Florentine painters seemed reluctant to break the Gothic-
tapestry tradition for landscapes. Their middle-distances rear up
alarmingly; we feel we could reach over and pluck figures from
far hillsides. Benozzo Gozzoli (1420-97) in his *Journey of the Magi*
(1459) shows a mechanical procession extricating itself from cliffs
and gulleys. But we feel less alarmed by the cramped perspective
when we know that the hills around Florence have that remarkable steep and intimate feel we get from paintings such as this.
It is probable that Gozzoli's purpose was not to please us with
natural beauty but to flatter the Medici family for whom the fresco
was made. Several of the Magi have a remarkable resemblance to
members of the Medici family.

While Masaccio was decorating the Brancacci Chapel with the
lively frescoes which were to precipitate Renaissance painting, a
Carmelite monk looked on. His name was Fra Filippo Lippi, born
in 1406 and a celebrated character and lady's man. He was a
prolific frescoist and developed Masaccio's style by softening the
lines and highlighting the features so that faces rather than whole
bodies became the centre of interest. The wide, clear features of
his *Madonna* (1452) anticipate the work of his student, one of the
most recognizable of Renaissance painters, Sandro Botticelli.

CHAPTER III

Technique becomes art

*Second generation of Renaissance artists - Piero della Francesca
and geometry - Pollaiuolo and influences from sculpture -
Mantegna - Botticelli and allegories - His decline - Development
of portraiture - Ghirlandaio - Piero di Cosimo - Contrary styles
of Early Renaissance.*

The years 1450-1500 are the years of the second generation of early
Renaissance artists, the sons of the founding fathers. Florence was
a wealthy city, heavily armed and ruled by the Medici family who
employed many artists. Paintings have by now developed from
being dull instructive decoration to being a means of free expression, but the artists cannot break away from the overworked
religious stories. The artists themselves had evolved from being
anonymous craftsmen and interior decorators to being respected
individuals, each with a portfolio of accomplishments. They have
freed themselves from the old guild system and have formed
academies of art. It is wrong to confuse them with more modern
models of an artist as an irrational and misunderstood genius
whose conceptions are ahead of his time. Renaissance artists
worked within the social structure. They had limited choice over
their subject matter and were bound by conventions of decorum
and tradition.

The new discoveries in perspective, colour, arrangement of figures,
of limiting the detail to significant action, of the use of shadow to
give depth, of imparting personality and emotion to figures, and
generally attacking a subject with a fresh creative determination,
put Florence ahead of other city-states. The local artists of
Siena, Bologna, Venice (where the Byzantine tradition continued
to be influential), Padua and Mantua, Urbino and Ferrara, all
adapted the Florentine manner. And of course the great Florentine
frescoists were spending long periods of their lives in Rome and
Siena by invitation.

Taking off from Domenico Veneziano's quick and lightly tinted
frescoes, Piero della Francesca (c. 1420-92) brought a mathematical
determination to the problems of perspective. He was something
of an outsider to the mainstream of Florentine art. It has been
suggested that he has been undervalued as an artist these centuries
because his sense of colour and geometry and his rather dry senti-
ments were out of step with the Florentine trend of sweetness and
emotion. His portraits of the *Duke of Urbino and his Wife* (1465)
are heavily worked in the Flemish tradition, perhaps because
Urbino had visiting Flemish painters who were competing with
Piero. The characters of the sitters seem remote from us, but are
to be respected for their authority.

A more characteristic painting is *The Flagellation of Christ* (1456-7).

The painting is divided up into geometrical space and the figures are arranged almost like statues. It must have been by some abstract theory and not by aesthetic consideration that Piero put the figure of Christ way back among distractions and under an eye-catching ceiling, while the foreground is taken up by three large figures, perhaps acting like an obtrusive chorus as in a medieval passion play. These eccentricities, coupled with Piero's devotion to treatises on painting and theories of shapes, put him on a plane with Leonardo da Vinci.

The first generation of Renaissance painters were old or dead, and the younger artists forming a second generation managed to throw off the lingering effects of Gothic-Byzantine painting, developing a kind of art which finds great favour to this day. Pollaiuolo (1431/2-98) was a Florentine sculptor known for his bronzes of lively groups engaged in athletic activity. He was reputed to have been the first artist to involve himself in dissection and anatomy as an aid to art.

With this knowledge he threw his figures into impossible contortions the better to demonstrate unnoticed muscles. *His Portrait of a Young Woman* (1465) illustrates a new direction, toward sensuous beauty of a kind that can be appreciated today. The young woman seems to be leaning back in a posture of earnest and trusting innocence, the sentiment previously reserved for a Madonna, and now distilled into an accessible, and we hope, sociable young woman. The painter has caught the sheen of the threads of her embroidered dress, and of her fine hair which is cleverly prevented from dominating her face. Technique has become art.

Mantegna (1431-1506) was a precocious young frescoist from Padua. His details of clothes and armour, buildings and weaponry fill his paintings with rare authority. But he went too far and painted flesh with sallow hues so that it resembles stone. He was a tenacious dabbler in perspective illusions, painting ceilings as if they were open to the sky, with figures peering down, and foreshortened figures to give a dramatically new view of over-familiar scenes. His painting of *The Dead Christ* (c. 1466) on canvas, continues to disgust and fascinate us. The painting is all the more real for the fine detail, the lines of the mourner's faces, and the holes picked in Christ's flesh. The painting was found in his studio after his death which suggests a strange morbidity within him, for he had the reputation of being a recluse in his later years. He had married the sister of the Venetian painter Giovanni Bellini and his influence reached Venice through the Bellini family.

In the rival city of Ferrara the painter Cosimo Tura (1430-95) was influenced by Mantegna to produce hard, metallic figures which also look back to Donatello. His *Virgin and Child enthroned* (1480) has a style falling far short of the Florentine painter's abilities. The Madonna's face owes more to Northern Europe and the whole disposition is overconsidered and mannered. He was a master of allegory, carrying parallel interpretation beneath nervous scenes of impetuous detail.

Sketch for an equestrian statue by Antonio Pollaiuolo
Munich, Staatliche Graphische Sammlung

16

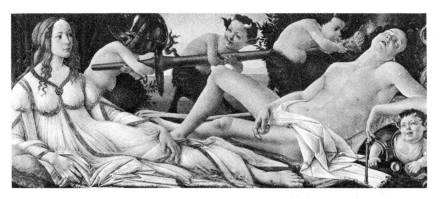

Venus and Mars, 1483
painting by Sandro Botticelli
London, National Gallery

Sandro Botticelli (1445-1510) was apprenticed to the colourful monk, Fra Filippo Lippi, who himself studied with Masaccio. It all leads us to realize with astonishment that a small and intimate group and its lineage produced the greatest movement in art of all time. Filippo Lippi was reported to have been stretched on a rack in order to extract a confession over the theft of his apprentice's wages, but it was probably not Botticelli who was cheated. Fra Filippo and his convent bride produced a son, Filippino, who became apprentice to Botticelli, and so the strands and threads of genius intertwine and reinforce each other.

Botticelli, coming at the very brink of the High Renaissance, lost by comparison, so that his reputation declined quickly after his death, not to be revised until the 19th century. And although his paintings excite curiosity rather than appreciation in the minds of art historians, there is something of great mystery about them that endears them to the public. His *La Primavera* (1477-78), with the cleverly arranged limbs and drapes of the figures setting up a compelling rhythm, like waves washing back and forth across the painting, and the delicate eroticism of the figures – a subject not alluded to by Victorian critics – shows a rare sensuality for a 15th century work.

The well-known *Birth of Venus* (c 1485) in which the lovely, un-muscled nude, coming ashore on a giant seashell, covers herself with her long hair, remains an impenetrable allegory upon a mythological subject.

Mars and Venus (1483) continues Botticelli's theme of mythology legitimising a soft eroticism. The hoofed putti (cherub children) are chaperones to a scene of rustic romance beloved by poets of the following century. The sleeping figure of Mars recalls Mantegna's *Dead Christ* but anticipates Michelangelo.

Botticelli found great favour with the 19th century group of painters called the Pre-Raphaelite Brotherhood. They appreciated the flat and linear style, and the eccentric Christian and Neo-Platonic allegory. Botticelli was reputed to have been an unstable personality who came under the influence of the magnetic religious reformer, Savonarola. His late work shows a regression and deterioration into distorted figures, decorative scenes and harsh colours. His *Mystic Nativity* is said to be a retreat and betrayal of the Renaissance style.

The closing years of the 15th century saw a quickening interest in the development of portraiture. Botticelli's angel from *The*

17

Mary Magdalene, 1505, detail
painting by Piero di Cosimo
Rome, Galleria Nazionale, Palazzo
Barberini.

Madonna of the Eucharist (1472) has the vague and cloudy expression of the time, seemingly untroubled by thought. The move to expressive portraiture was made possible by a move towards oil painting on canvas or board rather than frescoes. Flemish painters and paintings were finding their way into Florence to influence the local styles. Ghirlandaio's panel painting of *The old Man and a Boy* (c 1480) spells a tender relationship between the two figures, perhaps learned from the Flemish.

Ghirlandaio's obvious and anecdotal style was eclipsed by the next generation. Michelangelo may well have trained with Ghirlandaio and the Florentine eccentric Piero di Cosimo (1462-1521) was certainly influenced by him. Piero declared that he painted solely to please himself, and that he found inspiration from the stains on the wall. He painted mythological scenes as romantic fantasies. His *Death of Procris* (c 1490-1500) with the mortified satyr and perplexed dog set against a flat estuary has an effect of mournful desolation.

The variety of styles and contrary directions of the Early Renaissance were brought together by Leonardo da Vinci. These eighty years could be called a prologue to the High Renaissance. It was a time of rapidly mastered techniques, only occasionally blossoming into great art.

CHAPTER IV

Tell me if anything has ever been achieved?

False sentiment over Leonardo's early works - His virtuosity - Leonardo's design for figures - Anatomical dissections - Leonardo in Milan - "Virgin of the Rocks" - Workshop and scientific investigations - His notebooks - His return to Florence - Employed by Cesare Borgia - Map Making - "Battle of Anghiari" fresco - "Mona Lisa" - Unhappy stay in Rome - Invitation to France - His death there - Public appreciation of his personality.

The Virgin and Child with Saint Anne and John the Baptist drawing by Leonardo da Vinci London, National Gallery

Andrea del Verrocchio (1435-88) has been neglected for centuries. For a long time his reputation was based on the part he played as the teacher of Leonardo da Vinci. More recently a fuller evaluation ranks him as the most important 15th century Florentine sculptor after Donatello. Verrocchio was both an important link in a chain of influence and an innovator of a high order. He had learned his art, alongside Botticelli, under the celebrated friar Filippo Lippi, and he worked with Botticelli on several paintings.

Fra Filippo, we remember, had apprenticed his own son, Filippino, to Botticelli's tutelage. And it was to be the work of both Verrocchio and Filippino which had the greatest stylistic influence on Leonardo.

Verrocchio ran a large workshop which was a famous training ground for young artists. It seems that he was an inspired teacher, able to pass on the best techniques without destroying the individuality of his students. As a sculptor he invested his figures with great authority and set them in intimate, aggressive poses that reflect their latent social tensions. The full impact of this technique can be seen in Leonardo's *The Last Supper*, a wall painting in Milan, done with unconventional materials, that has nearly flaked away on that account. It is not the traditional line-up of disarming faces, but rather a tableau of reaching, gesticulating, active figures, made the more dramatic by the figure of Christ set against a window.

Leonardo, the illegitimate son of a peasant woman, was born at Vinci, outside Florence. At 15 he was apprenticed to Verrocchio's Florentine workshop where he learned painting and sculpture, as well as the technical side of art-production. The workshop of Antonio Pollaiuolo and his brothers was nearby and it is possible that the boy learned something of expressive posture and the use of anatomical dissection as an aid to dynamic realism in sculpture from Pollaiuolo. As a young man Leonardo was entrusted to add detail to the workshop paintings, designed and largely executed by his master.

Grotesque heads, c. 1495
drawing by Leonardo da Vinci
Windsor, Royal Library

On stylistic grounds it is believed that he painted the angel and a little landscape on Verrocchio's *Baptism of Christ* (c 1470-80). The angel on the left is found by some to have a greater realism and a sense of romantic grace, but we should arm ourselves against our own heightened appreciation of the angel's qualities. It is very easy to be prompted by prior knowledge of the painter and read special qualities into art objects. If we were falsely informed that the angel on the right was by Leonardo, we would certainly view it with equal reverence, and consider it far superior by comparison. Leonardo's paintings have a profound sense of mystery about them, which must seem to emanate from the paintings themselves and not be on account of sentiment over their creator.

Leonardo remained in Florence until his thirtieth year, and there he completed two *Annunciations,* a *Madonna and Child,* the *Madonna Benois, Ginevra de Benci, St Jerome* and the *Adoration of the Magi,* as well as a huge number of ink and pencil drawings, military sketches, diagrams of pumps, weapons and military apparatus!

The *Annunciation* in the Uffizi Gallery in Florence (c 1472) borrows from Verrocchio and may have had the participation of Lorenzo di Credi. It shows the probable hand of Leonardo in the accurate adaptation of a bird's wing for angels' wings, and in the folds of the Madonna's gown, for which he left sketches, but the painting has an archaic, almost Gothic feel, a sense of decorative ingenuity which has a weakened impact when compared to his later works.

The faintly exotic portrait of Ginevra de Benci (c 1478), captures, for Northern European eyes, the hair colour and distinctive features of a young woman from Northern Italy. There might be an ambiguous sexual resolution betrayed by the slight clench of the jaws and the close-focussing and narrowing of her eyes. She has a compelling personality. She makes us wonder what she is thinking, or, more accurately, what does she think of us!? It is sobering to realise how far painting had developed in the fifty years since Masaccio, and compare this with the slow progress in the five hundred years since this portrait.

The Adoration of the Magi (c 1481), abandoned as little more than an elaborate drawing, is remarkable now, as it was to Florentines in Leonardo's absence, by the arresting design – the figures grouped into a foreground pyramid – and the dynamism of the figures who bow, lean and crowd. Our eye is drawn involuntarily about the canvas from one figure to another. The painting of the emaciated *St. Jerome* indicates the influence of Leonardo's interest in anatomy. He claimed to have dissected 30 human corpses, which illustrates the Renaissance preoccupation with man as a complex and important source of emotions and reasons. Having no concepts of psychology and only the most simple mechanical analogy – clocks, and pumps – Leonardo attempted to understand man by close scrutiny and sketches. By this means he founded the important discipline of scientific illustration, but it requires more than descriptive analysis to begin to unravel the mystery of man the thinker.

1. Masaccio (Tommaso di Ser
Giovanni Cassai)
*The Expulsion of Adam and Eve from
Paradise,* 1425-27
Fresco, detail
Florence, Santa Maria del Carmine,
Cappella Brancacci

Masaccio's frescoes (wall paintings) in
the Brancacci Chapel are commonly
said to have started the Renaissance,
or rebirth of painting. Working alongside Masolino, a less talented
colleague, Masaccio developed the
move towards naturalism in painting,
started by Giotto a century before but
neglected since that time. This painting shows a considerable improvement upon the earlier style called
International Gothic. In the old style
the figures stood like a mute audience
to the central action. Masaccio
continued the same theme of familiar
religious events, but chose to illustrate
the human dimension. The full
human drama of a religious event is
marvellously expressed in the emotions
of the figures who weep and howl.
These frescoes marked such a startling development, that for a century
or more new painters flocked to the
chapel to study them.

2. Andrea del Castagno (next page)
David, c. 1450
Tempera on leather, 115x77x41 cm
Washington D.C., National Gallery of
Art

Following the thousand years of flat
and stylised paintings of religious
scenes, the painters of the Early
Renaissance looked back to Classical
Greece and Rome in order to redis-
cover the Classical version of Man,
anatomically accurate, active and
expressive. Castagno's *David* illustrates
the growing humanistic regard for
Man as a creature of emotion and
intellect, to be admired, not reduced
to a puppet of religious theory. The
new style of painting placed the
personality of man in the forefront,
and gave him presence and volume by
the use of perspective and shadow.
This humanistic interpretation of the
David and Goliath story rejects the
ritualised moral legend and sees
David as a vulnerable identifiable
person thrown into a dramatic
situation.

3. Masaccio
The Tribute Money, c. 1425
Fresco, 255x598 cm
Florence, Santa Maria del Carmine,
Cappella Brancacci

Masaccio, having decided that a group
of figures is far more than a collection
of individuals, set about developing
the gestures and mannerisms that
would unite the figures in a satis-
factory imitation of reality. He has
them interacting, arguing, moving
among each other. Visual integrity has
taken over from childlike structuring
of scenes in an orderly way. It represents a considerable intellectual breakthrough, probably even more significant to the development of painting
than the other techniques of
perspective and naturalistic lighting.
During the previous Gothic age
painting was essentially decorative.

4. Masaccio
Holy Trinity, 1426-27
Fresco, 680x475 cm
Florence, Santa Maria Novella

One of the first examples of strict
mathematical perspective in painting,
The Trinity also illustrates another
historic development, the use of
naturalistic lighting from an imaginary
single source. In previous styles, each
object or figure was illuminated,
indoors and out, from every angle.
Masaccio may have developed this
technique of naturalistic illumination
after studying the works of the
revolutionary sculptor, Donatello.

5. Sassetta (Stefano di Giovanni)
St. Francis renounces his Earthly Father,
1437-44
Panel, detail
London, National Gallery

The Early Renaissance was largely a
Florentine phenomenon and the other
city-states of Northern Italy continued

to be influenced by the International
Gothic master, Gentile da Fabriano.
In Siena, Sassetta may have been
impressed by the visiting sculptor
Donatello in the 1420's. He moved
away from the archaic and decorative
styles to reproduce his mystical
sacred visions in finely drawn and
luminously coloured paintings such

as this. There lingers more than a hint
of Fabriano's gothic style in the
compressed perspective and gold sky.
The painting also loses by the lack of
lighting scheme and absence of
shadows which confuses indoors and
outdoors, but it does have an interesting disposition of figures that
influenced later Sienese artists.

6. Paolo Uccello
The Flood, c. 1447
Fresco, 215x510 cm
Florence, Santa Maria Novella,
Chiostro Verde

Uccello's ostentatious demonstration
of perspective has all the appearance
of a glimpse down a mineshaft of
angels. His figures owe a clear debt
to Masaccio : they are developed as
sinewy, muscular and active, and
predate the sculptural and painted
figures of Pollaiuolo based upon his
anatomical dissections. Though not a
great painting *The Flood,* also known
as *The Deluge,* is remarkable for its
virtuoso demonstration of two
Renaissance techniques.

7. Paolo Uccello
*Niccolo da Tolentino at the Battle of
San Romano,* c. 1456
Panel, 182x317 cm
London, National Gallery

Uccello left Florence to do mosaic
work in Venice and was slow to take
up the new Florentine style. His
fascination for the problems of
perspective probably dates from the
publication of a book on the subject
in 1435. He was widely praised as a
master of perspective whilst conspi-
cuously failing to master the subject.
His backgrounds rear up abruptly and,
far from receding in an orderly
manner, they seem to owe a lot to
tapestry design with their compressed

depth and oversize multitudinous
figures. This painting, one of three
commissioned for the Medici Palace,
illustrates the pageantry and not the
reality of war. It depicts the victory
by the Florentines over the Sienese
in 1432.

8. Domenico Veneziano
Sacra Conversazione, 1442-48
Panel, 209x213 cm
Florence, Galleria degli Uffizi

Veneziano is reported to have brought from Venice to Florence some of the more delicate qualities of International Gothic. His paintings are characterised by light shades of green and pink, and a general lightening of the overall tone. This painting is suffused with a soft sunshine and has a rare harmony. This is one panel from a group from the St Lucy Altarpiece. It has a curious blend of Gothic and Renaissance; the Madonna sits in Renaissance architecture while the arches in the foreground have points in the Gothic style. Attempts by other artists to fuse Gothic traditions with Renaissance techniques were not so successful. Veneziano passed on his skills to his pupil, Piero della Francesca.

9. Fra Angelico
The stoning of St Stephen, 1447-50
Fresco
Rome, Musei Vaticani, Cappella
Niccolina

Guido di Pietro da Fiesola, called Fra
Angelico after his death as an appreciation of his art as much as his
saintliness and sweetness of personality,
was influenced by the Gothic traditions of decorative order, as well as by
Masaccio. Fra Angelico remains among
the more conservative of Early Renaissance painters for his innocent
rendering of holy scenes. He continued
the naive traditions of a previous
generation in which reality and
childlike conventions existed within
the same painting, and yet he drew
upon recent developments in the use
of colour and perspective. Fra
Angelico was a pioneer in landscape
painting, and is said to be the only
true interpreter of the Tuscan landscape.

10. Benozzo Gozzoli
Journey of the Magi, 1459
Fresco, Detail
Florence, Palazzo Medici-Riccardi,
Cappella

Gozzoli studied in the workshop of Ghiberti, and then with Fra Angelico. He began his career with Fra Angelico's religious feeling but moved to a more secular handling of religious events. This painting is part of four painted around the walls of the chapel under the close scrutiny of the commissioning Medici family. This painting can be compared with the best of the International Gothic, such as Gentile da Fabriano's *Adoration of the Magi.* Gozzoli makes a more determined attempt at a landscape perspective, and has made some progress, but he has not lost the tapestry convention of enlarging the more distant figures. He loved detail and developed an interest in cityscapes which he peopled with lively streetlife.

11. Fra Filippo Lippi
Virgin and Child with scenes from the life of St Anne, 1452
Panel, diameter 135 cm
Florence, Palazzo Pitti, Galleria Palatina

A larger-than-life figure in 15th century painting, this celebrated friar may have been the only true pupil of Masaccio. He was in residence when Masaccio was painting the Brancacci Chapel, and there is some small evidence that he might have been taught by Masaccio. As he matured as a painter, he was more influenced by Flemish painting and by the works of the sculptor Donatello. He adapted the convention whereby the Madonna on a large central panel was supported by saints painted on smaller side panels. He brought the figures together on one panel and experimented with a pyramidal arrangement of figures. He made early attempts to introduce movement into painting. It was reported that Botticelli was one of his pupils, and that Fra Filippo's son, Filippino, was later taught by Botticelli. The domestic scene to the rear of this Madonna has a Flemish feel to it, and the Madonna's expression is a move towards the expressions of intelligent ambiguity beloved by Leonardo da Vinci.

12. Piero della Francesca
Federigo da Montefeltro, Duke of Urbino and his Wife, c. 1465
Panel, 47x33 cm each
Florence, Galleria degli Uffizi

While Florentine painters were adopting a more realistic threequarter face view for portraits, Piero continued with the profile, a position well known from Roman portrait medals. In this instance, he has good reason, for the concealed side of the Duke's face and his hidden eye had been disfigured by an accident. The portraits, and the landscape background, which runs continuous from one painting into another, are markedly influenced by the Flemish, for Flemish painters were painting in Urbino while Piero was working there. Piero had lost a contract which went to Joos van Ghent and that might have stimulated him to learn from his competitor. The portraits themselves are less than impressive. There is something archaic and monumental about the figures; we are not invited to enjoy their personalities, only to be intimidated by their authority.

13. Piero della Francesca
The Flagellation of Christ, 1456-7
Panel, 59x81.5 cm
Urbino, Galleria Nazionale delle Marche

Piero studied under Domenico Veneziano, from whom he learned a Venetian sense of colour. He used colour successfully to suggest space and distance, but many of his original effects have been obscured, for the paintings have darkened with time. He was fascinated by the geometrical proportion which is reflected in the careful grouping of figures in his paintings. We are left with the impression that Piero's eccentric positioning of figures comes from some geometrical theory. The figure of Christ is pushed back to the middle distance – the smallest figure in the painting – and is obscured by the distraction of a heavily patterned ceiling and a statue on a plinth. The huge figures in the foreground draw our attention away from the distant ones. Most of Piero's paintings are found outside Florence, and this remoteness contributed to the decline of his reputation; that is, until this century.

14. Antonio del Pollaiuolo
Portrait of a young Woman, c. 1465
Panel, 52.5x36.5 cm
Berlin-West, Staatliche Museen, Gemaldegalerie

Antonio Pollaiuolo and his brother Piero ran a highly successful workshop in Florence where they produced sculpture, painting, and pursued many lesser crafts such as embroidery. They were particularly concerned with representing movement. They were reported to have been among the first painters to study anatomical dissection as an aid to true representation of figures in action. This portrait setting and the stark contrast of translucent white flesh tones against a dark blue background go a long way towards capturing individual expression and personality. The significance of her very tilted pose is lost to us now, though it does reveal to us a great expanse of white neck. This serves to break the unsatisfactory convention of a small head fixed upon a sculptural mass of decorative clothing. So much more of her personality is revealed in her posture.

15. Andrea Mantegna
The Dead Christ, c. 1466
Canvas, 68x81 cm
Milan, Pinacoteca di Brera

Mantegna was a highly individual genius who was heavily influenced by the Classical styles of art. His paintings are characterised by backdrops of classical architecture captured in alarming perspective by the detailed painting of armour and artifacts, and by dramatic illusions of foreshortening. This last technique is well illustrated by this painting, which also accentuates the rather metallic flesh tones and the features he may have copied from the sculpture of Donatello. The painting has a cold morbid realism which strips away the dreamy, ritualistic tradition of the crucifixion and reveals simpler horrors of desecrated flesh.

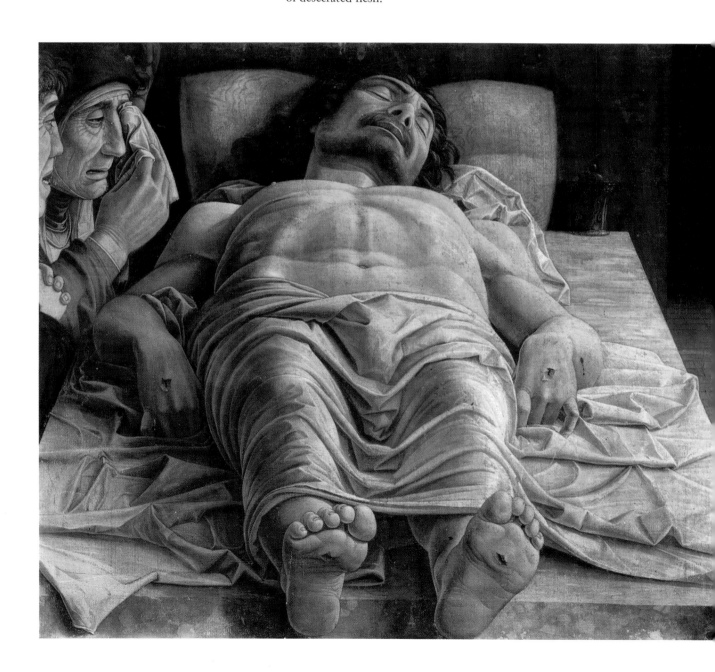

16. Cosimo Tura
The Virgin and Child Enthroned, c. 1480
Panel, 239x102 cm
London, National Gallery

Mantegna's style influenced Cosimo,
who was the court painter in Ferrara,
and Cosimo's colleagues, Francesco
del Cossa and Ercole de' Roberti.
Cosimo's style is characterised by
sharply metallic figures, a good deal of
distracting detail and crinkled
drapery. The effect is awkward and
decorative. Clearly the Ferrarese style
was no match for the Florentine one.

17. Sandro Botticelli
La Primavera, 1477-78
Panel, 203x314 cm
Florence, Galleria degli Uffizi

Botticelli has set his lively Renaissance
figures against a stylised Gothic forest.
It is a difficult painting to interpret
for it has been inspired by literary and
philosophical reflections all contained
within a framework of allegory. It
does seem however to be an attempt
to reconcile Neo-Platonic theory,
fashionable at the time, with
Christian ideology. Putting all this
aside, the painting has a sensuous
naiveté and is widely appreciated as
a celebration of dance and the
beauties of the countryside. There is
a marvellous sense of weightlessness
and movement, something transpa-
rent and fluid about the composition
which releases it from the artist's
intention that it should be decorative
philosophic instruction.

18. Sandro Botticelli
The Birth of Venus, c. 1485
Canvas, 175x278 cm
Florence, Galleria degli Uffizi

Again this most celebrated painting
has a mythological and an allegorical
meaning which is best neglected in an
appreciation of a most compelling
composition. There can be little doubt
that this Venus, coyly covering her
nakedness and with a faraway look,
was commissioned from Botticelli to
satisfy the erotic interests of a patron.
Venus had to play the double role of
goddess of earthly love and a window
into the Divine, and served as a
vehicle for the depiction of the female
nude until later generations could
allow themselves to paint nudes
without the mitigating explanations of
their purpose. It would seem that
Botticelli's nudes were the highest
achievement of this particular style of
painting in which an outline of a
figure is filled in with colour. Under
Leonardo da Vinci's brush the figures
become shadowy masses, given
weight and volume by the use of
subtle lighting effects.

19. Sandro Botticelli
The Madonna of the Eucharist, c. 1472
Panel, detail: The angel's face
Boston, Isabella Stewart Gardner
Museum

Throughout this century, the
unacknowledged development in the
treatment of saints and angels, was
aimed at the depiction of character
and personality in a face. It was as if
each artist had to improve upon the
conventions, and then the public had
to adjust to the new improvements.
This angel has a neutral and
unexpressive look, and is surpassed
by the work of Leonardo at this time.

20. Domenico Ghirlandaio
Portrait of an old Man and a Boy,
c. 1480
Panel, 62x46 cm
Paris, Musée National du Louvre

Ghirlandaio worked with Botticelli and others under the direction of Perugino to decorate the walls of the Sistine Chapel in Rome. He would introduce contemporary customs and faces into his frescoes, and though his easy-on-the-eye prosaic style made him popular in his lifetime, his work is thought to lack imagination. This portrait of a man with a strawberry nose, caused by a common ailment of the time, is remarkable for the tender relationship shown between the man and the boy. It was thought that Ghirlandaio was then heavily influenced by Flemish painting.

21. Piero di Cosimo
The Death of Procris, c. 1510
Panel, 65.4x184.2 cm
London, National Gallery

Piero had a sentimental idea of history; he painted popular little scenes depicting the discovery of fire, wine or honey. He was a notable eccentric and in his claim that he was sometimes inspired by the shape of stains on the wall, he was expressing an advanced idea of the artist as a person uniquely sensitive to the visual world. This painting of accidental death, set against the background of a pale estuary, is said to strike a mood of mournful desolation.

22. Andrea del Verrocchio and Leonardo da Vinci
The Baptism of Christ, 1470-80
Panel, detail
Florence, Galleria degli Uffizi

Andrea del Verrocchio ran a large and successful workshop in Florence where one of his apprentices was Leonardo da Vinci. The angel on the left is believed for stylistic reasons to have been painted by Leonardo, and the story goes that, upon seeing how superior it was in delicacy and charm to his own, Verrocchio swore to give up painting. His pupil was just eighteen at the time. However there are problems of attribution in Renaissance painting, of knowing who painted what, and if this angel were discovered to be by another artist, its special qualities might disappear.

23. Leonardo da Vinci
Ginevra de Benci, c. 1478
Panel, 103x75 cm.
Washington D.C., National Gallery
of Art

This haunting portrait beautifully
illustrates Leonardo's concern with
the mental life of his subjects - their
personality, their thoughts and their
emotions. The expression on the face
is open to many contradictory
interpretations but most people
register pride and a certain sexual
ambiguity, neither inviting nor rejec-
ting but rather, in the act of deciding.
When we consider that this painting
came some fifty years after Masaccio,
we may then appreciate the astonishing technical advances in that
time, and also consider the slow
progress in the five hundred years
since then.

24. Leonardo da Vinci
The Virgin of the Rocks, c. 1480
Panel 197x119.5 cm
Paris, Musée National du Louvre

A very similar painting, now in
London, was completed some
fifteen years later. The painting is
a revolutionary collection of all the
best Renaissance techniques, bound
up with Leonardo's own technique of
'sfumato' – the gradual shading off of
shadow, like smoke. The dramatic
backlighting of the figures to give
them volume (at last we are no longer
distracted by folds in cloth!), and the
harmonious disposition of the four
figures all give the painting a rare
depth and complexity. The careful
depiction of flowers and plants all
come from Leonardo's natural observations.

25. Leonardo da Vinci
The Last Supper, c. 1495
Fresco, 460x880 cm
Milan, Santa Maria delle Grazie

It was sculpture, and not painting,
which developed dynamic tension
between a number of figures, and
Leonardo must have seen this
technique demonstrated in the
sculpture of his master, Verrocchio.
Though it has badly flaked, and is
now barely visible having been painted over by several later artists, *The
Last Supper* is a masterpiece of imagination in the variety and interplay of
characters. From the gestures alone
we are able to build up a clear picture
of each man's thoughts. It is not just
a number of familiar biblical figures
identifiable by their styles of painting;
many of these characters are identifiable by their personalities.

26. Raphael
The Madonna of the Chair, c. 1514
Panel, diameter 71 cm
Florence, Palazzo Pitti, Galleria
Palatina

Raphael was skilful in adapting the
styles of his masters, synthesising new
techniques and investing his work
with a special kind of sweetness.
This painting, though technically
very accomplished, projects senti-
ments quite out of step with the
Renaissance humanistic view of
passionate, thinking man. The
sweetness is seen, not only in the
expressions, but in the softening of
the outlines and the pneumatic
children.

27. Raphael
The Muses, 1508-11
Fresco, Detail from *The Parnassus*
Rome, Musei Vaticani, Stanza della
Segnatura

About as far from Michelangelo as
possible, these frescoes have an easy
accessible style. The colours, textures,
folds and hues of cloth invite the eye
into the painting and entertain it. The
muted gestures, the calm expressions,
the spring of water and the instru-
ments suggest a very chaste and
orderly kind of pleasure, in keeping
with church painting. We are left with
the feeling that Raphael's figures
never argue; they always discuss.

28. Michelangelo Buonarroti
The Holy Family, 1503-04 (Madonna
Doni)
Panel, diameter 120 cm
Florence, Galleria degli Uffizi

By the age of 25 Michelangelo had
completed the marble statue of the
Madonna and the dead Christ, called
The Pietà, now in the St. Peter's. He
was primarily a sculptor and his paintings, with their balanced and
muscular figures have rather too much
of a sculptured quality. After
Raphael the figures in this painting
seem garish and vulgar. The naked
men of the background are a little
overbearing, and the painting is saved
by the expression of paternal
concern on the face of Joseph, which
softens a rather uncompromising
treatment of this theme.

29. Michelangelo Buonarroti
The Creation of Man, c. 1511
Fresco, detail
Rome, Musei Vaticani, Cappella
Sistina

Michelangelo must have been
familiar with Classical treatments of
this theme, and also with attempts by
his near-contemporaries, notably
Uccello – to portray Adam. But these
figures have become the definitive
representation of God creating Adam,
in the popular imagination. It was a
very bold conception to treat this
most dramatic of religious stories
with apparent casualness. A reclining
Adam lifts a limp and langourous arm
to receive the spark of life. One would
have expected a more auspicious
beginning for mankind – but
Michelangelo was right. His depiction
of the very spark of creation without
the accompanying melodrama leaves
each generation free to consider the
astonishing implications of Creation.

30. Michelangelo Buonarroti
The Delphic Sibyl, 1508-12
Fresco
Rome, Musei Vaticani, Cappella
Sistina

The pagan equivalents of the old-
testament prophets, painted at inter-
vals along the ceiling, give authority
to the story. The sibyl has a graceful,
asexual look about her, for Michelangelo had little interest in painting the
female nude.

31. Michelangelo Buonarroti
The Last Judgement, 1536-41
Fresco, detail
Rome, Musei Vaticani, Cappella
Sistina

After a long gap Michelangelo was
invited back to complete the painting
of the Sistine Chapel. This time he
decorated an end wall with a huge
and vigorous painting of this most
disturbing religious event which
tormented him in a personal way. The
floating figures scramble up into a
judgement or fall back to hell.
Christ, no longer aloof, becomes part
of the scene raising his hand to
condemn, and devils carry off the
unfortunate.

32. Jacopo Bellini
Christ in Limbo, c. 1440
Panel, 29x58 cm
Padua, Museo Civico

The Bellini family, beginning with
the father Jacopo, are the principal
founders of the Venetian Renaissance
school of painting. Jacopo began his
working career in imitation of the
old Gothic masters, but while
working in Florence his style changed
to an imitation of Masaccio. His paintings have a stiff and static quality,
and this one is marred by a studio
conception of the appearance of
rocks. No doubt old Jacopo provided
the ideal workshop conditions for his
sons to lift art to something interna-
tionally recognized.

33. Giovanni Bellini
Sacred Allegory, c. 1490
Panel, 73x119 cm
Florence, Galleria degli Uffizi

Said to be the most inventive of painters, Bellini, inspired the atmospherics
of his own city, developed a skill for
setting his scenes in a soft, powdery
light. This inspired handling of
illumination became a hallmark of
Venetian Renaissance painting ; it was
said that one can tell the season and
even the hour of the day from an
outdoor scene painted by Bellini. This
painting of a ritual conducted before
the Byzantine church of San Marco
develops another theme which
became distinctively Venetian, the
cityscape.

34. Giovanni Bellini
The Doge Leonardo Loredan, 1501-05
Panel, 61.5x45 cm
London, National Gallery

This finely detailed portrait is possibly
the best by Bellini. The art of portraiture had developed with Bellini and
Leonardo to such a level that we feel
confident to assess character from the
appearance alone. Most people see
wisdom and authority tinged with
mercy, but not the less tangible
qualities of uncertainty and sensitivity
to be seen in Leonardo's portraits.
Bellini's Doge is the painter's
equivalent of a sculptured bust.
The next step would be to show
hands and arms.

IOANNES BELLINVS.

35. Bartolomeo Vivarini
Madonna and Child enthroned, surrounded by Saints, 1465
Panel, 118x120 cm
Naples, Museo e Gallerie Nazionali di Capodimonte

The Vivarini painting family contributed, with the Bellini family, to the distinctive Venetian style. Their early works have the distinctive decorative quality of the Byzantine-Gothic. Following contact with Mantegna about the time of the painting, Bartolomeo's work showed distinctive improvement.
This painting is too fussy and ornamental and there are disconcerting faults with perspective on the lower steps. The richly woven dress of the Madonna is a distinct improvement upon the usual distracting folds of red cloth, and the faces of the saints have a measure of character.

36. Pisanello
Portrait of Ginevra d'Este, c. 1443
Panel, 43x40 cm
Paris, Musée National du Louvre

Pisanello continued the earlier tradition of painting called the International Gothic. He came from Pisa, trained in Verona but went to work in Venice where he painted frescoes in the Doge's Palace which have since been destroyed. He was among the first artists to draw from nature rather than copy the works of others and this portrait is decorated with flowers and butterflies drawn from his close observations. The portrait itself is somewhat lifeless as if it had been carved as a relief in stone. We can only hope that it flattered the young woman who sat for it.

37. Antonello da Messina
St Jerome in his study, c. 1460
Panel, 47.7x36.2 cm
London, National Gallery

This Sicilian painter came to Venice with a feeling for superior Flemish coloration. He was said to have had a profound influence on Venetian painters, bringing a sense of interior volume and space, and demonstrating the technique of using colour shading to indicate mass and volumes. His portraits are exceptional, and his *Portrait of a Man* (1475) was said to have been widely admired. Antonello brought a Flemish sense of detail to his work, which was now possible with the change from frescoes to oil painting. This picture with its detail down to the words in books and the birds through the window, was easily confused with the work of the renowned Flemish artists Van Eyck and Memling.

38. Vittore Carpaccio
Scene from the Legend of St Ursula, 1495
Canvas, 281x307 cm
Venice, Gallerie dell'Accademia

Carpaccio worked as an assistant to Bellini in Venice, but developed his own distinctive style. He has been praised for his wealth of naturalistic detail and for his narrative sense in retelling the stories of the saints. He was among the early Venetian painters of townscapes which culminated in the later works of Francesco Guardi and Canaletto.

39. Giorgione
Fête Champêtre, c. 1510
Canvas, 110x138 cm
Paris, Musée National du Louvre

Giorgione, a pupil of Bellini, was one
of the first to produce small oil paintings for private collectors. Little is
known about his personal life apart
from the fact that he was a great
innovator who profoundly influenced
Titian but died of the plague in his
early thirties. He did memorable reclining nudes and also outdoor paintings
having an indefinable and oppressive
mood. In this work the glowing areas
of flesh are balanced by sunlit meadow
and bright foliage. The landscape has
a softly-contoured and antique feel
about it which, with the low cloud,
forms a powerful sense of a particular
location.

40. Titian (Tiziano Vecellio)
Bacchanal, 1518-19
Canvas, 175x193 cm
Madrid, Museo del Prado

Titian is often regarded as a founder
of modern painting. He lived into his
nineties and was able to capitalise on
the new ideas of Giorgione after his
early death. He was reputed to have
been a rapid painter who worked on
several paintings at once and used his
fingers instead of brushes on the final
stages. This painting illustrated the
effects of the wine from pleasure
through drunkenness to sleep. It has
a lighthearted feel about it compared
with the exaggerated gloom of the
Mannerist school which was developing in Florence and Rome at this
time.

41. Titian
Venus of Urbino, 1538
Canvas, 119.5x165 cm
Florence, Galleria degli Uffizi

Titian may have taken the idea of a
reclining Venus from an earlier painting by Giorgione which was
completed by him. Having made the
break from religious themes, the
painters held to mythology as an
intermediate stage before daring to
portray quite imaginary figures, made
up from studio models who would
come and pose for them. This Venus
has little of mythological significance
and is best appreciated as a beautiful
and inviting young woman of the
town. The figures of the background
act as a kind of chaperone to offset
her inviting look.

42. Titian
Self portrait, c. 1562
Canvas, 86x65 cm
Madrid, Museo del Prado

Titian developed the type of official
portrait which was taken up later by
Rubens and Van Dyck. In these stern
features we can read the practised
determination which enabled him to
run a workshop and produce so many
paintings.

43. Correggio
Jupiter and Io, c. 1530
Canvas 163.5x74 cm
Vienna, Kunsthistorisches Museum

Correggio, from the city of Parma,
developed a characteristic soft style
which anticipates the next era of
painting, the Baroque. He did notable
frescoes and like Mantegna he
painted ceilings as if they were
heavens full of saints and angels.
This painting in which Io is seduced
by Jupiter who had turned into a
cloud, has a splendid erotic quality,
slightly shocking, and quite arresting.
He was a fine painter who managed
delicate effects with a skilful application of paint so that it was said to
have been condensed on the canvas.

44. Parmigianino (next page)
The Madonna of the Long Neck, c. 1534
Panel, 216x132 cm.
Florence, Galleria degli Uffizi

Influenced by Correggio, Parmigianino
went on to develop the new style
of painting called Mannerism which
relied on the effects of exaggeration,
distortion and conflict. This famous
painting with the enormous Christ-
child sets a mood of disruption and
confusion. The small and distant
figure on the right comes of a new
fashion for using perspective effects
to make strong contrasts in size. The
painting is lively but is not lovely, for
it seems to have been done quickly
upon an ill-considered and hasty
composition. For the Mannerists, the
composition and subject matter was
of less importance than the eccentric
way in which it was presented.

45. Angelo Bronzino (next page)
An allegory of Time and Love, 1545-46
Panel, 146x126 cm
London, National Gallery

This arresting and vulgar painting
with its obscure allegory has the
Mannerist characteristic of contorted
postures and an overcrowded canvas.
The stonelike figures are without real
expression and the painting engages
our interest but fails to gain our
sympathies. Bronzino was a court
painter to the Medici family and is
known for his cold and stylised
portraits.

46. Jacopo Bassano
Susanna and the Elders, 1571
Canvas, 85x125 cm
Nîmes, Musée des Beaux-Arts

One of a Venetian family of painters, Bassano was swayed by many influences but maintained his love of solid figures set in a gloomy landscape, often mountains in a storm. He used peasants and animals and piles of fruit or household utensils to fill out his religious compositions. This work with its hastily painted figures and dark background, looks toward the Baroque.

47. Tintoretto
Nativity, 1576-81
Canvas, 538x465 cm
Venice, S. Rocco

Tintoretto drew heavily upon the style of Titian but added the types of figures he admired in the work of Michelangelo. In the Mannerist tradition, the central theme of the painting is moved aside in favour of the more dramatic effects of the setting, the derelict roof, the scattering of straw and the peacock on the hayrake. The painting seems hurried and careless. It may be that Tintoretto's design was finished by his students and his children, which would have been necessary for him to complete all the paintings he was commissioned to do.

48. Paolo Veronese (page 60)
Mars and Venus united by Love,
1576-80
Canvas, 205.7x161 cm
New York, Metropolitan Museum of Art, Kennedy Fund

Veronese marks the closing years of the Renaissance with accomplished paintings often with Classical ruins in the background. The story of this painting is unclear, but the figures are not so strange as to defy appreciation. There seems to be a new feeling in the painting as if it registers a move away from the inner tensions of the Renaissance painters to a state of decorous indulgence. The scene is one of great intimacy but would have been so much the better without the intrusion of the putti – the cherub children. The woman has removed her dress after having come from a background of courtly civility to meet the tanned and rugged soldier.

In 1482 Leonardo went to work for the Duke of Milan in the more pragmatic atmosphere of that city, for Florence was bedevilled – and many artists mesmerised – by some mystical medieval theories called Neo-Platonism. Clearly he hoped to be engaged in some taxing projects in the brilliant court of Ludovico Sforza. He remained there for 17 years and painted *Lady with Ermine,* a *Virgin of the Rocks,* and the mural *The Last Supper.* He devoted many years on the ambitious designs for a monumental equestrian statue of Francesco Sforza. There are many sketches; a full-sized clay model was made, but the bronze could not be spared from the casting of cannons, and the statue was never finally cast. Nor had Leonardo mastered some severe technical difficulties in casting such a large piece. Perhaps Leonardo has given the world of art a new means of exhilaration and torment, art that defies technological skill for its making.

There are two full-size versions of *The Virgin of the Rocks,* one in the Louvre, and one in London, completed some 15 years later. It is difficult to know why an artist so sparing of his painting talent should have reproduced his own painting, although the later London version is a little more mature and more considered. For its masterly design – the harmonious arrangement of four figures – for the serenity of pose and expression; for the luminously soft figures placed against a formation of back-lighted rocks, the paintings represent a startling, and very moving development.

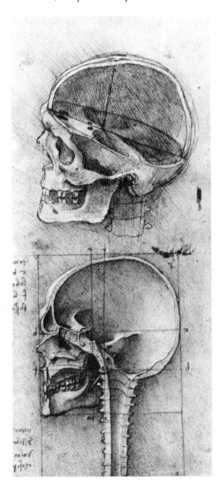

The skull, detail
drawing by Leonardo da Vinci
Windsor, Royal Library

It is well to remember that the paintings of the High Renaissance grew to huge proportions. We may be intimidated by the absorbing sense of involvement we feel while standing before such huge canvasses; it is an experience quite unlike that of examining reproductions in books. The paintings of Leonardo in particular have a mystery and impact which is all but lost in reproductions. While in Milan, Leonardo managed a workshop and introduced apprentices to his methods. He gave time to treatises on painting and architecture, on mechanics, anatomy, botany and it seems, upon everything from tanks to forerunners of the aeroplane and bicycle. He wrote volumes on his thoughts and observations; left-handed and in a backwards writing which can be read only with a mirror. His monologues, addressed to an imaginary reader, have a rich and vivid vocabulary which uses Italian, not the usual Latin, for a scholarly work. This contributed to the development of the Italian language for scientific prose. And throughout his notebooks – heavily illustrated with sketches of everything from grotesque faces observed on the street to the pattern of flowing water – the melancholy line "Tell me if anything has ever been achieved?" is so often repeated. His was a lonely and unconfirmable quest for understanding.

About the turn of the century, Leonardo returned through Mantua and Venice (where he advised on fortifications against the Turks) to Florence. Again he seemed not to find a satisfying project. He completed a *Madonna* (now lost) and began another *Virgin and Child* before entering the services of the violent adventurer and son of a Pope, Cesare Borgia, there to meet the prophet of

Mona Lisa, 1503-05
painting by Leonardo da Vinci
Paris, Musée National du Louvre

unscrupulous politics, Machiavelli. Cesare Borgia, much younger than Leonardo, forced Northern Italy away from the restrained system of military alliances into savage battles involving treachery and assassination. Could there have been something the artist found attractive in the tyrant's personality, or did he see a chance for a new, outrageous project? Leonardo found himself engaged in charting cities and making topographical plans (and by these efforts he would seem to have founded the skill of cartography) before drifting back into Florence in 1502.

More grandiose plans (to divert rivers and build a canal connecting Florence to the sea) all sketched in charming detail, but never completed. In 1503 he was commissioned to paint a fresco of the *Battle of Anghiari* in the Palazzo Vecchio, opposite a wall on which the younger Michelangelo was to do another battle scene. Leonardo developed a violent, interlocking design of men and horses, contesting together in the thick of battle. He tried new fresco techniques. The colours ran into one another and the project abandoned, leaving just sketches of how it would have been. It was the time of the world's most famous painting, *La Gioconda,* called the *Mona Lisa.* She haunts us all. She thinks, and she does not live. Again, Leonardo demonstrates an impossible abstract principle of the visual arts, that an intricately developed design imbues an object with fascinating depth. The personality of the painter seems to fuse with, and give personality to, a representation. The many hours of preliminary sketches are distilled into a humanising imitation of personality.

By 1506 Leonardo is back in Milan working on *Leda and the Swan,* the *Virgin and Child with St. Anne,* and the second, London, *Virgin of the Rocks.* He gives time to an unfinished equestrian statue, and he fills thousands of sheets with sketches of anatomical dissection: muscles and the position of the foetus in the womb. He believes that a mystical force and motion, operating under orderly and harmonious laws of nature, shape all things, whether it be climatic or anatomical. It remains a curiously primitive notion; more in keeping with ancient Greece than with modern thought.

During his last years (1513-19) he stayed by invitation first in Rome, where his talent was neglected while Raphael and Michelangelo were engaged in significant commissions; then in 1516 at Cloux in France. He painted *St. John the Baptist,* designed festivals and did his greatest drawing of a floating figure and a vision of the end of the world, the deluge. He died at Cloux in 1519 and his grave was destroyed and lost in the French Revolution.

One of the greatest painters of all time dabbled in painting almost as a minor hobby. His contributions to painting by way of example were a revelation. Through the centuries his unique, secretive, yet creatively audacious personality has made him an attractively sympathetic father-figure to artists and scientists alike.

CHAPTER V

Florence goes to Rome

*Perugino - Influence on Leonardo and Raphael - Raphael's
synthesis of styles - Raphael invited to Rome - Michelangelo - His
move to Rome - The "Pietà" and "David" - First commission
for the Sistine Chapel - Work on tombs - At the mercy of
patrons - Second commission for the Sistine Chapel - Large
frescoes - Michelangelo as an old man - His final works and his
death - The pessimistic mood of his paintings - Andrea del
Sarto - His portraits - Fra Bartolommeo - His influences.*

A fellow student of Leonardo's at the Florentine workshop of
Verrocchio was a young painter from Perugia, from whence his
name, Perugino. As his own style matured he brought a cool
objectivity to the Florentine style, which was tending toward
exaggerated realism. His figures were calmer, with more modest
gestures and less distracted expressions. It took some time for
the new sense of Umbrian restraint to permeate the local styles
Perugino may well have influenced Leonardo, and showed him
how to contain the tension behind figures of emotional complexity.
Perugino is best remembered as a teacher to a seventeen-year-old
painter of minor devotional paintings from Urbino, called
Raffaello Sanzio, but known as Raphael (1483-1520). Raphael
moved from a sweetly religious style to imitate his master,
Perugino with near perfection. The young Raphael learned to
distribute his gentle little figures through the architecture with
less formality than Perugino, while keeping the grand perspecti-
ves. It was an essential modification of his master's style, and one
which found favour with the public. Having overtaken his master,
he moved from Perugia to Florence in 1504.
Raphael was a thorough and determined student, whose skill was
in selecting the best techniques of his contemporaries Leonardo
and Michelangelo, and his predecessors right back to Donatello
and Masaccio, to bring about a synthesis of styles. He may be seen
to have been a popularizer of the High Renaissance.
The great commissions for art-works were not so forthcoming
in Florence. In Rome the Pope Julius II was attracting the best
artists to the monumental task of rebuilding the Vatican. By the
architect Bramante's suggestion Raphael was invited to Rome in
1508 where he found immediate acclaim for his easy and pleasing
style. It represents a kind of impersonal, colourful and uncontro-
versial compromise in an age of striving genius and idiosyncratic
paintings.
The painting *The Madonna of the Chair* (1514), though sensitive
and charming, represents a kind of regression to another, sentimental era of painting. The figures are painted with great skill
and an advanced sense of naturalism, and yet they do not delight

La belle jardinière
drawing by Raphael
Paris, Musée National du Louvre

Madonna with the goldfinch, c. 1506
(Madonna del Cardellino)
painting by Raphael
Florence, Galleria degli Uffizi

in the humanistic sense of mankind as intelligent and emotionally complex. It might be unkindly said to be a chocolatebox style. *The Muses* (1508-11), detail from a larger composition, illustrates his rapid and popular style in which the figures harmonize and add to the general feeling of optimism. It is a sharp contrast to the work of Michelangelo. Raphael's lack of personal commitment, one might say integrity, might explain why he was chosen by Pope Julius II to interpret the philosophical scheme for a series of frescoes in the Stanza della Segnatura. The theme was the historical justification for the enormous powers of the Catholic Church. Through Raphael's designs the Church is seen to be the culmination of historic processes and the natural repository of the truth. The important fresco of the series, *The School at Athens*, is a masterpiece. The whole cycle represents the highest achievement of a painting done purely for the purposes of decoration and propaganda. It is untaxing, and effortlessly fascinating. Upon his early death in 1520 the Papal Court honoured their lyric painter for his contribution to the ideological respectability of the Catholic Church. In his favour it should be said that Raphael's last work, *The Transfiguration* was done in a more vigorous and agitated style which looks forward to the next age of painting, the Baroque.

The direction of painting may well have been derived from Raphael's grand and sentimental style if he had not been overwhelmed by a contemporary, Michelangelo, who chose to excel not only in painting but in poetry, architecture and by universal acclaim in sculpture. He was born in 1475, and led such a public life that he is better known, through letters and his own writings, than any other artist of that time. He grew up in Florence and was apprenticed to Ghirlandaio. Before he was twenty he was forced to flee to Rome on account of his association with the deposed Medici family. He might have seen Rome as a fresh and untried field for a new artist when he arrived there in 1496, by way of Bologna. But Rome was also a frontier of enterprise and duplicity.

Though he toyed with classical subjects, his sculpture turned to religious themes, especially with his marble *Pietà*, the Madonna looking upon her dead son, which remains the jewel of St. Peter's basilica. He returned to Florence in 1501 and in 1504 completed the huge marble statue of *David* for which he is best known, a statue out of all scale to the visiting public, and considered sublime by some and vulgar by others. It was highly regarded by the new democratic commune of Florence, who commissioned him to paint *The Battle of Cascina,* on a wall, across from his rival, Leonardo. Michelangelo crowded the space with versions of his contorted male nude, but the wall and the painting were later destroyed.

Pope Julius II summoned Michelangelo to Rome and had him devote reluctant years to a huge sepulchre of many figures. The next year this determined sculptor found himself under contract to paint the ceilings of the Sistine Chapel. The sculptural qualities of Michelangelo's paintings are apparent

Pietà, 1499
marble by Michelangelo
Rome, St Peter's

in the determinedly three dimensional volume of his figures, and the frequent clustering of figures with many points of contact necessary to give strength and rigidity to sculptural groups.

This may be seen in *The Holy Family* (c 1503-4), in which we may feel a desire to turn the figures around and view them from another angle. He spent four years on this first commission for the Sistine Chapel, painting pre-Christian prophets and pagan sibyls. The detail of the *Delphic Sibyl* (1508-12) shows a figure of lightly muscled and marble-like beauty. This asexual female form may have been to his liking. He liked to paint virile young men, and it is believed, since he addressed love poems to both men and women, that he was bisexual by nature.

The vanity of his patrons set him for years designing and sculpting family tombs; the usual Renaissance pattern of genius as the handmaiden of privilege. Often a death in the family or decline in their fortunes meant that the years invested in a project had to be abandoned. At one time he was subject to such demands from two patrons that he complained that he did not have time to eat. All the more surprising that he had time for his literary interests. As if looking purposely back to another age for a genius who was his equal in creativity, he took to Dante the poet, and proposed to the Pope that he should build a new tomb for Dante. But the tombs of the powerful and unscrupulous took precedence, and the project never attracted patronage. Michelangelo's interests, divided between Florence and Rome, were threatened when the Pope and the Spanish Emperor combined forces to attack the Florentine Republic. The sculptor found himself on the defense committee for Florence, and abhorring the rhetoric of politics, he fled the city for Venice and was declared a traitor. But he was forgiven and returned to complete the Medici tombs.

A new Pope, Paul III, appointed him official sculptor, painter and architect to the Vatican and in 1536 he began work on *The Last Judgement* in the Sistine Chapel, where he had worked before. It is the most celebrated and astonishing of frescoes; a great sweep of figures, rising up to judgement or tumbling back to hell. The figures are detached from any setting and are expressive in themselves. Michelangelo with one assistant worked upon the painting for five or six years, and he was over 65 when it was completed. His own writings reveal that *The Last Judgement* had a personal meaning, for he felt himself a sinner, and hoped to be worthy of salvation.

Michelangelo turned wearily once more to the unfinished tomb of Julius II, when he felt that he had lost his youth and manhood. It was finished, reduced in size, and is known for the startling statue of *Moses,* with rays of light springing from his head like horns. There followed two large frescoes, *The Conversion of St. Paul* and *The Crucifixion of St. Peter,* which reveal the depths of his religious torments. His poems, written through this time are concerned with his doubts and fear of death. At the age of 75 he was beginning the *Pietà* for Florence Cathedral. The figures are formed but the work is not completed. Often he would sculpt the essential figures and leave the work to be finished by assistants.

David, 1501-03
marble by Michelangelo
Florence, Galleria dell'Accademia

Young man, 1523
drawing by Andrea del Sarto
London, British Museum

As an old man he had autocratic powers in the Vatican workshop and angered assistants with his fixed opinions. Changes in Popes moved him swiftly in and out of favour, and he suffered the humiliation of having his naked figures "clothed" by the Counter-Reformationist determination of Pope Paul. His last years were given largely to architectural design. Among his drawings was that for St. Peter's cupola or external dome (1557-58). And in his last days he threw himself into one or two more "pietàs" (the descent from the cross and the pathos of a dead Christ in the Virgin Mary's arms). He had complained about his imminent death 48 years before it was to happen of a probable stroke, at the age of 89 in 1564, the year of Shakespeare's birth; he is buried beside the cenotaph of Dante in Santa Croce in Florence. Michelangelo remains the most important and influential sculptor of all time. The Renaissance began with the influence of an architect and a sculptor and a frescoist, Masaccio, and reached its high points as the three disciplines became one, within the genius of one man. It may be that sculpture and painting had now to be separated, to develop in different directions.

The greatest painter of the generation, after the celebrated three, was Andrea del Sarto (1486-1530) who studied under Piero di Cosimo and responded to the innovations of Leonardo and Michelangelo. His work, especially his treatment of landscapes, has all the realism of the Flemish. He was a painter of high originality who spread dramatically gesturing figures through spacious landscapes. Though a skillful and energetic colourist he turned to monochrome frescoes, perhaps as a result of current artistic theories. He is particularly noted for his portraits and for his drawings, and from these he would seem to stand between Leonardo and Titian.

Lorenzo di Credi who began his painting career alongside Leonardo, developed no more than a modest talent. Lorenzo, like Botticelli, had been intimidated by Savonarola's anger at the revival of pagan culture, but had gone further and destroyed most of his work. Fra Bartolommeo (1472-1517) painted in the style of Perugino but was also influenced by the death of Savonarola to give up painting for a while. After a trip to Venice he took up some techniques from Giovanni Bellini; after a visit to Rome he was influenced by what he saw in the Sistine Chapel. He continued the High Renaissance style even after Mannerism had taken over as the predominant style.

CHAPTER VI

The early Renaissance in Venice

Jacopo Bellini - His son Giovanni Bellini - Venetian handling of light - His influence - Vivarini - Byzantine influence in his work - Pisanello - Antonello da Messina - His influence on the Venetian style - Carpaccio - His handling of light - Interest in painting cities - Giorgione - Titian - Correggio.

Venice saw the growth of a separate branch of the Renaissance. Jacopo Bellini (1400-70) began his career in the imitation of Gentile da Fabriano, the leading International Gothic painter in Italy. But he was impressed by the Florentine styles of Masaccio and Uccello so he journeyed to Florence and returned to his native Venice with the new style of which *Christ in the Limbo* (c 1440) is an example. He retained Byzantine or Gothic characteristics such as rich decorative colouring and gold-filling for backgrounds. One of his daughters married Mantegna and his sons furthered the cause of the Renaissance styles.

Giovanni Bellini (1431-1516) fell under the influence of Mantegna and was later to be affected by Flemish painting. His *Sacred Allegory* (1490) has rather more of the lingering Venetian Gothic in its array of figures but it indicates his skill in handling the powdery and diffuse Venetian sunlight which makes that city ethereal today. It is said that one can tell the season and the time of day from the incidence of light in a Bellini painting. It was Bellini who was to take up oil painting and develop the qualities of the illumination in his works by the technique of thin, translucent layers. The celebrated portrait of *The Doge, Leonardo Loredan* (1501-05) does not invoke the human qualities of intelligence and fallibility as Leonardo would have liked, but the awesome qualities of patriarchal wisdom and the strictness born of absolute authority.

With his gift for investing landscape with soft, golden light he developed the style for his students Giorgione and Titian, as well as the later Venetian painters Lorenzo Lotto and Carpaccio.

Antonio Pisano, called Pisanello (1395-1455) from Pisa, who began his career in Venice, was among the first of painters to draw from life rather than continue the medieval tradition of copying from other works. Most of his drawings survive as a valuable record for the study of styles and techniques of the time. The portrait of Ginevra d'Este (c 1433) has some of the finely observed detail of flowers and butterflies resulting from his observations. He also drew animals (his horses are well known), plants, costume design, perspective drawing, as well as designing medals.

Bartolomeo Vivarini (1432-99), a member of one of Venice's influential families, developed an austere and characteristic style which was to form, with Bellini, the Venetian style. The

Portrait of a boy
drawing by Antonello da Messina
Vienna, Graphische Sammlung
Albertina

Madonna of 1465 well illustrates the eastern influence of elaborately decorated material and Eastern Orthodox seriousness which formed the Byzantine echo ringing through Venetian Early Renaissance painting.

It is suggested that the growing interest in oil painting was stimulated, particularly in Venice, by a Sicilian, Antonello da Messina (1430-79). The predominant Venetian technique was to build up form with lines and shading. To that he added his own style, which was to build up form with colour. There is something decidedly Flemish about his style, married to the Italian spatial virtuosity (the many, defined side-chambers and compartments) apparent in the early painting *St. Jerome in his Study* (c 1460). It is said that while residing in Venice other painters conspired to discover the secrets of his technique for portraits, of which he was a master. His *Portrait of a Man* (1472) has a rare naturalism that seems of another era of painting, and proved very influential. Vittore Carpaccio (c 1460-1525/26) was heavily influenced by Antonello and by the Bellini family. His *Scenes from the Legend of St. Ursula* (1495) show his great originality, his handling of light (which was to become a leading Venetian characteristic), and a satisfying wealth of detail. He was to start a Venetian fashion for painting cities, taken up by Canaletto and Francesco Guardi. Giovanni Bellini in Venice closely paralleled the style of Madonnas developed by Raphael in Florence and Rome. But Venetian painting, in the hands of Bellini's students Giorgione (c 1477-1510) and Titian (c 1489-1576), moved toward new directions of compelling and atmospheric subtlety. Giorgione was an enigmatic master of the Renaissance who died aged only 34, and whose paintings were often completed by, and confused with, Titian's. He invested his paintings with a poetic mood and a gentle pastoral lyricism by the use of idealised form, colour and light. The celebrated *Fête Champêtre* (c 1510), or Pastoral Concert, is a remarkable synthesis of techniques. If we need evidence for Vasari's statement that Giorgione was profoundly influenced by the visit of Leonardo to Venice in 1500 it might be seen in this painting. Titian, a fellow student, was heavily influenced by Giorgione, and on this account their unsigned paintings are easily confused. His huge and highly praised *Assumption* (1516-18) made his name, but though there is a masterly handling of diffused and redirected light, the painting loses by its stern iconography (overprecise religious scheme) and by the confusion of minor figures, the tumble of putti lifting the Virgin upon a cloud, and the crowding faces encircling her. However, Titian had a Venetian taste for pagan and hedonistic mythological subjects. His *Bacchanal* (1518-19) illustrates his imaginative handling of figures. He shows restraint in the postures and natural gestures and has no time for the emotional tensions and forced styles of Mannerist painting which became the fashion about this time. This idyllic world is founded upon humour and the pleasures of the mind and body. The bright cloud and shadowy foliage tell of a world of variety and surprise, not one of unremitting gloom proposed by Mannerist painters.

Two boys in a landscape, c. 1505
drawing by Titian
Vienna, Graphische Sammlung
Albertina

Portrait of Charles V, 1548, detail
painting by Titian
Munich, Alte Pinakothek

Titian developed great skills as a portraitist and was commissioned
to paint many powerful men in armour or in chains of office. He
wears his golden chain of Knighthood in his own *Self Portrait*
(c 1542), presumably done with two mirrors so that he can catch
a profile unfamiliar to himself which allows him to paint
objectively his own intelligent face. He painted many beautiful
and erotic nudes; the famous *Venus with a Mirror* and the *Venus
of Urbino,* (1538). This last painting was inspired by Giorgione's
earlier *Venus* in which a landscape was later added and a stray
putto expunged by Titian. Giorgione's *Venus,* though chaperoned,
has an inviting expression. Both paintings, unspoiled by a more
deliberate erotic intention which took hold of the later painters
Boucher and Fragonard, remain timeless classics. Titian's work
demonstrates the vital and enhancing influence of Classical art
and mythological subjects in a world which remains intimidated
by the authority of religious subjects.
The ideas of the High Renaissance grew in other cities, notably
in Parma, and in the hands of Antonio Allegri, known as
Correggio (1494-1534). Some of the ceiling frescoes with their
dramatic illusions (turning the inside dome of the Church into the
vault of heaven) strongly anticipate a later style of painting, the
Baroque. His mythological works such as *Jupiter and Io* (c 1530), in
which Io is seduced by the cloud, have a fulsome, erotic quality. He
treated his subject matter with great confidence, and with a delicate application of paint which seems at times to have been
condensed onto the canvas.

69

CHAPTER VII

Late Renaissance and Mannerism

Spread and character of Mannerism in painting - Parmigianino - Improvement upon nature - Pontormo - His style - Rosso - His style - Bronzino, court painter - "Allegory" - Bassano - His styles - Anticipating the Baroque - Tintoretto - Veronese - The durability of his style.

There remains the Late Renaissance, a period of some eighty years when a new style of painting developed as a reaction to Leonardo's cool and studied compositions. Originating in Rome and Florence and spreading to Northern Europe, the new style, now called Mannerism, explored the possibilities of exaggeration, distortion and conflict. Each artist assumed the right to express his idiosyncratic manner. In the race to be different and shocking, the artists chose distortion of space and figures, bizarre systems of symbols or allegory, startling colours, dreamlike fantasies, improbable compositions in which the supposed subject is lost behind minor figures, displays of muscular nudes, distortions in perspective and a general crowding and overloading of the picture space.

It was said that when Raphael died his soul passed into the body of a talented young painter who came to Rome bearing three pictures and the name of his birthplace. Parmigianino (1503-40), one of the initiators of the Mannerist style. He was probably a pupil of Correggio, but borrowed techniques from others. His famous *Madonna of the Long Neck* (c 1535) with its elongated figures and rampant limbs (and its school-age baby Jesus!), illustrates a characteristic of his work, the search for an improvement upon nature in the proportions of the human body. He died young and left a collection of excellent drawings.

Jacopo da Pontormo (1494-1557), also called Carrucci, pupil of Andrea del Sarto, produced works of nervous and emotional intensity as well as a number of portraits. He borrowed from the celebrated Albrecht Durer whose engravings were circulating in Italy at this time. His *Deposition* (c 1530) is remarkable for the crowding of brightly-coloured but essentially weightless figures floating in some timeless ritual.

Giovanni Battista Rosso (1495-1540), a friend of Pontormo went further with the expression of great emotion. His *Deposition* has a stark, overpowering mood achieved through a simple style and bright colours that could be found in a comic-book. Rosso was invited to work in France and his influence spread from there.

The works of both Pontormo and Rosso find great favour among contemporary art critics for their affinities with the 20th century style called Expressionism.

A pupil of Pontormo, Bronzino (1545-72) broke away from his

Half figure of a seated man drawing by Jacopo da Pontormo Florence, Galleria degli Uffizi

Head of a young woman
drawing by Veronese
Florence, Galleria degli Uffizi

master's style to develop one of his own. His portraits are both decorative and impersonal, as befitting a painter of the Medici court. We see his love of obscure allegory in *An Allegory of Time and Love* (1545-46), with its stony asexual nudes in contorted poses. It is an icy possibility, stemming from Michelangelo's neglect of personality in painting.

Jacopo or Giacomo da Ponte (c 1517-92), known as Bassano, found his way through many of his contemporaries' styles without developing one of his own. He began by absorbing the styles of Giorgione and Titian in Venice but returned to his native town of Bassano where he developed an interest in portraying the peasants in rustic settings. *Susanna and the Elders* (1571) reveals an unimaginative setting done with quick brushstrokes and set in

71

Male nude
drawing by Tintoretto
Florence, Galleria degli Uffizi

an atmospheric gloom which anticipates a preoccupation of the Baroque painters, and of Tintoretto.

Both Jacopo Robusti (1518-94), known as Tintoretto, and Paolo Veronese (1528-88) drew from the style of Titian, and each went on to influence a different style and development. Tintoretto set as his ideal the fusion of two great influences; drawing from Michelangelo and colouring from Titian. As Tintoretto was deliberate and pessimistic so Veronese was flamboyant and joyful. Veronese, from Verona, was attracted to the charm of Raphael whose work he admired on a visit to Rome. He established himself as a popular decorative painter in Venice, and brought a secular interpretation to religious events.

Tintoretto made his reputation with *San Marco rescuing a Slave* (1548) and went on to decorate the Doge's Palace, and to give many years to the frescoes of the *Scuola Grande di S. Rocco* in Venice. He drew extensively on the Mannerist techniques of foreshortening and of receding diagonals, and the sporadic use of illumination to highlight some figures and hide others. Tintoretto's *Nativity* (1576-81) illustrates his quick, distracted style and the imperfect use of highlights on the forehead and shawl. Tintoretto was assisted by his children and by apprentices to help him complete an exhausting schedule of religious commissions. His portraits of old men are reported to be masterly revelations of an inner spark of fiery resolution.

Veronese's heavily populated paintings set historic subjects against a background of Classical architecture. He was employed to decorate the Ducal Palace of Venice, where he used skilful foreshortening to make the figures appear to float in space. In his decoration of a villa, Veronese turned the ceilings into skies and the walls into landscapes adorned with classical ruins. He loved to paint amusing detail (jesters, dogs, a servant with a bleeding nose) and he was brought before the Inquisition for despoiling a holy painting.

Veronese finished many fine allegorical tables, and left behind a huge collection of drawings when he died. *Mars and Venus United by Love* (1576-80) illustrates his gift for gathering his figures in a harmonious rhythm, and with a great authority and confidence. His style has never lost favour. It was to dominate Venetian painting through a further century of imitators, and then to have considerable impact on 19th century painting.

Bibliography

The author has consulted the following works in the writing of this book.

The Art of the Renaissance *by Peter and Linda Murray*
The High Renaissance and Mannerism *by Linda Murray*

The Lives of the Painters, Sculptors and Architects *by Giorgio Vasari*
Renaissance and Baroque *by Heinrich Wölfflin*
High Renaissance *by Michael Levey*
Leonardo da Vinci *by Kenneth Clark*
The Notebooks of Leonardo da Vinci *ed. by Irma Richter*
Michelangelo *by Howard Hibberd*

Raphael *by James Pope-Hennessy*
Mannerism *by John Shearman*
The Renaissance in Italy *by John Hale*
Encyclopaedia Britannica has useful short biographies and articles of the Renaissance painters.